OBLIVIOUS

A VEGAN MEMOIR

SANDE NOSONOWITZ

COPYRIGHT

Print ISBN: 9781096389194

Book design by Sande Nosonowitz
Cover graphic design by Jen Barbato
Front cover photo by Nandhu Kumar
Back cover photo by Night Owl

For the animals.

The fate of animals is of greater importance to me than the fear of appearing ridiculous; it is indissolubly connected with the fate of men.

— ÉMILE ZOLA (1840-1902)

CONTENTS

Oblivious

It's too normal not to notice;
It's too easy not to ache.
So simple not to suffer,
Too willful not to wake.
How dare we not bear witness
To the torture at our door,
To deny that we're complicit
In the slaughter on that floor?
We yield the knife that severs life;
We stop a heart that beats;
Then go about our busy day.
I mean, everybody eats.
Ah, but that's not true, for some are starving
And die of hunger's scourge
While men in suits and ties and boots
Throw back a few, pick up a fork and knife — and gorge.
The grain it takes to feed that steak could feed a child instead,
But that is just not how it works. That's just not why they're bred.
Profit steers this dirty ship. Our leaders jump on board
To subsidize this evil sin, just as they fund our wars.
It's systematic cruelty. It's legal and endorsed.
But it's torture and it's slaughter, and we all must pay the cost.
We're hypnotized, indoctrinated, and it's all so god-damned scary
We wash down our compassion with a two-pint glass of dairy.
Don't look away, don't hide your eyes:
Their slaughter is surely hideous.
The only thing that could be worse
Is to remain oblivious.

- Sande Nosonowitz

INTRODUCTION

Let the truth exist somewhere other than inside your body.

— DELLA HICKS-WILSON

We take the long road or the short one. Sometimes we get there, sometimes we don't. We conform to the norm or we break out of the mold in which we've been confined. There's a point of connection between us, as individuals, and the whole. Whatever we do affects the world around us, and that's the most difficult concept to grasp: our lack of separateness. Our egos refuse to let us see this most important part of a peaceful life's cycle. This is why so many stay comfortably in the mold, while others break out of it. And for a few outliers, the mold unexpectedly shatters, leaving shards scattered, and hearts in flames, burning with the desire for change.

I finally realized, after four years of trying to write this book, that the reason I desperately wanted to write it, was so that this truth, my truth, would have another place to reside, other than inside me. At first, that might sound selfish, and I'd agree that, in part, it is. Nevertheless, if my story touches you at all, the waves of truth will ripple out into the world, and change it, too.

Filled with the usual doubts of a first-time author, I retained the help of a writing coach, Marissa -- an adorable, smart, sassy millennial from Canada. She pulled this book out of me, week after week, gently holding me accountable for writing it. We didn't know each other at first, but that changed within a few weeks. She'd listen to my impassioned pleas for the animals, the sadness I felt for the fate of the earth and the comforts, as basic as clean air and fresh water, that my grandchildren may never know. We talked about our health. She opened up to me about physical problems she'd experienced, as I shared mine. And then, something happened that removed the bullies in my head that were telling me that I had no right to write a book about my journey, that no one would want to read it, that it would make no difference at all. Three and a half weeks into our work together, I received this email from my coach:

Hi Sande!

My partner and I were able to watch What the Health *last night -- thank you for recommending it. We discussed this in depth, and we've decided to transition to vegan. We're both fully on board, and there are just so many reasons, let alone our health and general moral conscience, to give it a real shot. And I'm very excited about having your support for the transition. Cheers! -- Marissa*

I cried when I read this. My passion had an effect on someone else. I helped someone make the connection with my words. That's all I needed to motivate me week after week until the six letters "The End" hit the bottom of the page. It was exhilarating for me, knowing that she was personally prompted to make a major life shift, and that I'd played a part in it. Marissa had her synapse moment, just as I'd had mine, except I was present to witness hers.

If you're vegan and reading this book, I hope you can relate to the moment you made the connection. And if you are not vegan, my deepest wish is that you read these pages and connect with something I've written that sparks the fire of your own transformation. The compassion is already inside us; we just need to uncover it. It takes courage. We've been buried in illusion, but each of us can take off our armor of defensiveness and replace it with the armor of liberation, of rising stronger.

FIRST FORAY

Sometimes when you're in a dark place it feels like you've been buried — when you've really been planted.

— CHRISTINE CAINE

I had my nervous breakdown in a Chinese restaurant. It was right in front of my new husband's family and patrons and waitstaff and anyone passing by walking their dog along the Hudson River trail next to the China Rose in Rhinecliff, New York. There's a Metro North railroad track right on the riverfront, and I suppose someone on their way up from New York City, head angled in just the right position, could have caught a glimpse of the meltdown that was about to change everything.

My nervous breakdown took on a life of its own. I could feel it traverse its course from my echoing gut, up through my thundering heart, hover over my throat for a good two minutes before making a beeline to my brain, waiting for it like a catcher, opening his mitt, anticipating a fastball.

My breathing was labored and tears had begun to stream down my face without sobs or sound. I looked over at Stevan's cousin, Susan. She knew that something was about to happen, being an intuitive psychotherapist and all. But did I know that every sorrow, every grief, every empty yesterday would erupt through those chakras they talk about in yoga, intensifying as it ascended for release? A volcano of emotions held, something to do with time, so much lost time.

I felt myself cracking open. I could hear my own thoughts: "Not one more day! I am not going to spend one more day unfulfilled, not even one more day." My heart pounded. My head felt as if it was in a vice. There was a tender voice in me that grew into a raging bellow, screaming: "This is not enough! There has to be a deeper way to live. I should be doing something more meaningful, something bigger than me, bigger than this." Then, what was borne of silent tears became a broadcast of hyperventilation and cries of unlocked anguish.

There was a dog I used to hear in the distance when I'd take walks near my home. I tried desperately to follow that sound to his (or her) rightful house and save that poor dog from a life of confinement. How could one creature compose such a wild cry for help in the suburbs of Poughkeepsie? Who was allowing that sound to permeate a whole neighborhood? I now had something in common with this imprisoned canine and we were singing in two-part harmony tonight.

Susan, ever empathetic, immediately began to show her calm concern. Kevin, her significant other, was on standby – concerned, but letting Susan take the lead. Stevan was obviously upset and uncomfortable, but dug in to try to comfort me or, more accurately, to fix things. Husbands tend to want to fix things. Luckily, my aging mother-in-law and father-in-law were at the far end of the table and were not aware that their only daughter-in-law was in the midst of a major meltdown.

The agony of being an unfulfilled seeker had reached its peak. I was at a breaking point. As I sat around the table at the China Rose, drinking my mojito, looking around at everyone immersed in their own thoughts, their own dinners, I tried to tune into my breathing, but could only hear the frantic beating of my heart. I looked around the table at these people who already loved me, their hearts beating at their own pace and pattern, while mine was desperate to be heard.

The most telling experience of the evening came when I realized that most of the family and all the servers and other patrons, were oblivious to the whole thing. I felt myself literally and audibly unraveling in front of everyone, and yet all around me laughter and chatter and appetizers were the way of things. Either completely unaware or perhaps unable to process feelings as uncomfortable as these, most of the people around me seemed not to notice anything unusual.

"Guys: I'm practically convulsing. Does this not warrant a brief pause?" I didn't say that, but how could they not know? Whatever their reasons, I suddenly felt confused about the ability that some of us, maybe all of us, have to ignore another's suffering. This was the first time I'd thought about how the mind deals with the misery of another, and how differently we process it. How are we able to be oblivious to suffering, when we know it's happening right in front of us? My nervous breakdown suddenly shifted to an inversion of perspective, after which nothing would ever be the same.

My heart rate decelerated. My breathing slowly returned to normal. I wiped my tears away with the white linen napkin, took a big sip of my mojito and, in silence, ate my cashew chicken.

2
_____

YOGA

Yoga is the journey of the self, through the self, to the self.

— THE BHAGAVAD GITA

S o, what exactly do you do after a breakdown? I went back to the country club where I worked as a marketing and membership director, but every free moment I spent in the yoga studio. I breathed in and I breathed out and I tried to answer the poet Mary Oliver's question, "Tell me, what is it you plan to do with your one wild and precious life?"

Practicing yoga, I felt calm and invigorated at the

same time. I liked it. And since yoga is a space and practice for self-discovery, I replaced the batteries of my inner flashlight and went to work.

I had a teaching degree from the State University of New York at Stony Brook, but aside from doing some teaching in Arizona where I lived after college, I never used that piece of paper very much. I had dozens and dozens of jobs at different times in different places, but my career never felt stable. I thought of it as eclectic: marketing, advertising sales, video producer -- and single mom, one tough gig to be sure. I attached my identity to all of the jobs I had, only to end up feeling disappointed and disengaged at some point. This happened every time, but I didn't recognize a pattern. Yoga was teaching me to release my attachments. Yoga showed me I was good enough now, without reaching the pinnacle of what my ego thought success might be. It was freeing and I bathed in the feeling as often as I could.

Stevan was as supportive as he could be, and although he couldn't grasp what this self-discovery trip was all about, as my husband and partner, he wanted me to be happy (and probably wanted me to be a bit more normal, too.) After college and law school, he had put out a shingle and slowly embarked on the law career he practices to this day. One job – only one job. Kind of blows my mind.

One day in yoga class during *savasana*, relaxation

pose, it came to me. If this is where I can feel calm and invigorated at the same time, then why not do what I love? I'm going to be a yoga teacher! There was a yearlong training starting in six months and I signed up.

The next day I gave my boss six months' notice. Who does that? Six months. I knew what I wanted and I wanted to give him time to find just the right person to fill the job I was really good at, if I do say so myself. I thought that was the yogic thing to do.

If I'd started this practice in my twenties or thirties, the physical aspect of yoga would have been a breeze. But I was in my early 50s and "Oy!" was now a regular term in my vocabulary and it's not Sanskrit. But *ahimsa* is.

The first book we were required to read in yoga teacher training was *Jivamukti Yoga: Practices for Liberating Body and Soul*, by Sharon Gannon and David Life. I always thought our teachers might have started us off with somewhat lighter reading. This book was intense and summarizing it for our monthly essays was no small chore. Chapter 4, "Ahimsa; Walking the Nonviolent Path," was about yogis who live a vegan life. I remember saying to myself, "Why the hell is she telling me what to eat? What does this even have to do with yoga?"

When I look back on those thoughts now, my whole being cringes. I love chapter 4 and read each word with deep awareness. But back then, in the autumn of 2007, I chose to skim through that chapter and was relieved when that book was over and done. No connection made – zip, nada. But onward I went on my merry yogic way, because it felt so damned good. And I wanted to share it with the world.

In June of the next year, I got to do that. I graduated yoga teaching training at the studio in Rhinebeck, New York, with a flower wreath in my hair and my husband and stepson watching. If their eyes were rolling into the back of their skulls thinking about the fact that they were related to an old hippie chick trying to find herself, I didn't notice. I was so happy they were there with me. I was going to make something of this training. I was a yoga teacher. (Well, I was. Sure, they'd taught me to let go of identity attachment, but a little won't hurt.)

I was euphoric to be out of the corporate grind and doing something I believed could change the world. I started teaching yoga at a few different studios and loved every single minute of my new life. I thought back to all the days and years I spent stressed out at work, and how I might have managed it if I'd had yoga in my life then. I suddenly came upon the idea to teach corporate yoga, to take those stressed-out souls and quiet their minds and stretch their hunched-over bodies during their busy days of making money for someone else without a shred of appreciation. (Whoops, I didn't intend to make this about my experience, but here we are again.)

Back to school I went to get certified to teach corporate yoga. With engines revved into sales mode, I was convincing midsize and big businesses to let me inside their buildings to teach their employees. Banks said yes. So did government agencies. Even notoriously buttoned-down IBM. One corporate client led to another and I was teaching ten to fifteen corporate classes a week, even hiring teachers for certain clients. Was this the pinnacle of what I had been searching for? I thought it just might be.

3

THE 'US' GIFT

Some of our greatest historical and artistic treasures we place with curators in museums; others we take for walks.

— ROGER CARAS

We were coming up on our 10-year wedding anniversary -- no small feat for a soul-seeking hippie and a divorce lawyer. "So I was thinking about a few ways to celebrate our anniversary," Stevan mused one night at dinner. "I wanted to run them by you."

Intrigued, I answered, "Okay, let's hear them."

"Well, you have three choices. A *you* gift, an *experience* gift, or an *us* gift." One suggestion he gave for the *you* gift (meaning a gift exclusively for moi) was cosmetic dental work. I had been whining about wanting a whiter and more appealing smile. This would be a gift solely to quench my ego's desire and it was very tempting.

The experience gift was a trip we would take together and I'd choose the place. I'd been rambling about Telluride, and how I yearned to return there. Never mind that it would take two planes and a three-hour drive to get there, but I knew it was worth the aggravation.

Then came the *us* gift – something for the both of us to enjoy together. "The *us* gift, the *us* gift, the *us* gift!" I blurted out as loudly as I could, clapping my hands like a six-year-old who's just been told she's going to Disneyland. I knew just what the *us* gift was because we had been talking about getting a dog for a long, long time. Well, actually, I was the one talking about it, whining about it, selling him on the idea time after time after time. My persistence paid off after ten years, as we were finally getting a dog. The *us* gift.

Instead of opting for a rescue, we chose to buy a puppy from a breeder. I was tasked with researching yellow lab breeders. We'd decided on a yellow lab, because of temperament and the fact that my son had a yellow lab whom I'd looked after during the workday for about a year. The other reason was because yellow labs are so darned cute.

The first breeder I called was Carla. After our first conversation, I knew that we were going to get our dog from her. I'm an impulsive person and I can't lie about that. I just really liked her style and her willingness to really talk to me about this process. Most people want to answer your questions and get off the phone. Carla spent over an hour talking about how she got into breeding dogs, what her life was like, and she was interested to know about me because she cared about where her puppies were going and with whom. We scheduled a visit right away and I could not wait to get there.

Driving up the long driveway to her house, I could feel my heart racing. The love inside me was bubbling up and about to overflow. And when we actually saw the puppies – well, this level of cuteness ought to be illegal. Stevan and I gushed and hugged and cuddled and ooohed and ahhhed while the puppies played and ran and jumped into our arms. Then they did the sweetest thing. They ran in a circle and all at the same time, the puppies just dropped down and fell asleep. Every single one of them at the same exact time. My heart dissolved inside my chest. I asked Carla which one she would pick for us. She picked up a little guy with a black collar that read, *Bad to the Bone*. "This one," she said. "He's spunky, curious, and affectionate." We were in love.

It was hard to fathom waiting eight weeks for this precious soul to be part of our family, but that was the rule. We drove home giddy and excited. We laughed at ourselves while discussing how big the father's head was. I told Stevan that he would have to love this dog no matter how big a head he grew into. He agreed and we moved on to picking out names. Again, I went into research mode. We settled on the name *Henry*. It means "ruler of the home." We thought that would be appropriate.

The day finally came to pick Henry up and bring him home. All the accessories and necessities were in place. Two crates – one the size of a Manhattan studio apartment. I didn't want him to feel cramped when we went out and had to leave him home. Toys, food, bedding, and books (those were for us) were all waiting in a designated spot in our newly doggie-proofed house. Life was about to change. We were ready. Or so we thought.

The first few days were hectic and my inexperience was obvious. I was at the point in my life where I was free. My son, Jason, was living abroad and my stepson, Daniel, had just finished college and had a job and apartment in New York City. I could do whatever I wanted. But wait. This adorable little creature was taking up every waking minute, and I felt guilty leaving him alone. Tired, cranky, and torn between pangs of love and twinges of resentment, I longed for my freedom. Days passed and I became unhappier and more annoyed about this huge new responsibility. Looking back, I had developed a serious case of *post-puppy depression*. A few weeks in, I told Stevan that I couldn't handle this – it was just too much. I phoned Carla and told her what I was going through. She told me I could bring Henry back to her and they would find him a home, presumably with no problem.

The next day, I packed up his crates, food, toys, blankets and bedding, and Henry and I were headed back to Germantown. I cried every second of the forty-five-minute drive. I sat in Carla's kitchen and cried for another half an hour. She was kind and understanding, but I'm sure she was thinking I was a total nut job.

I paced back and forth in her kitchen while she held Henry. I had to call Stevan. I needed guidance. I was so confused. I dialed the phone. "What should I do?" I asked between loud sobs and trying to catch my breath. Stevan didn't want to give Henry back, but I was the caregiver every day while he was at work, so he wanted to leave the decision up to me. "But what should I do?" I couldn't get myself to physically leave the house without Henry.

I carried his crates, toys, food and bedding and

packed them back into my car. I took Henry in my arms and walked down the driveway – we were on our way back. The tears I cried every second of the 45-minute drive home felt different from the ones I'd cried on the way there.

I was giving it my best shot and sought out advice from trainers, behaviorists, and experienced dog people. I was trying, but it wasn't enough. I still felt overwhelmed, and I didn't know how to shake this feeling. Stevan's friend told him about a family who was interested in getting a dog. They had three kids and 80 acres of land. He told us to bring Henry over to meet the family and see if that might be a solution to this crazy dilemma.

A few days later, after a heavy winter snow, we brought Henry to this beautiful place to see if we should give him to this family. The family's young kids were all over the prospect of getting a puppy. They were chasing Henry around the house, the youngest throwing his tiny toy soldiers at him while squeals of delight could be heard in harmony from all the children. We stayed awhile, and then we were asked to leave Henry there for a couple of hours to get acquainted. I walked from that house in a trance, looking back a few times in what felt like slow motion. As Stevan and I drove out of their driveway, an incredible wave of clarity washed over me in an instant. Something had changed. I turned to Stevan and uttered these five words as indignantly as I felt them, "They can't have my dog!" The dark cloud of my post-puppy depression had lifted – dissolving and transforming into a love affair that would alter the trajectory of my life forever.

4

THE INJURY

You desire to know the art of living, my friend? It is contained in one phrase: make use of suffering.

— HENRI-FREDERIC AMIEL

A t this point in the journey, my little Upstate New York town was finally living up to its name, Pleasant Valley. I was gratefully aware of what a good place I was in. I loved my home, my dog, my thriving yoga business and my husband --not necessarily in that order. There was peace in creating my potted garden in late spring and in the summer meditation workshops I took at the Omega Institute. Autumn arrived and I reveled in my favorite season, standing in the backyard with Henry, watching the golden leaves fall like rain. Thanksgiving was my favorite holiday then, all about gratitude and family and hugs and food and wine.

Early December brought cold air and hot soup. Winter brings bone-chilling days where I'd yearn for greenery and sunshine. I caught a bad case of bronchitis that month and had to move into the guest room for three nights. My incessant coughing was waking Stevan who gets up at 5:45 to start his day. I missed him. I couldn't sleep and I resented him because he could. Three nights with no sleep was taking its toll on me, so I left a message for my doctor and asked him to call back as soon as he could. This doctor was notoriously difficult to reach, especially because his gatekeeper was difficult and argued, no matter what you said to her or how nicely you said it. I felt as if she was always doing me the biggest favor by allowing me to make an appointment with my doctor. I wondered whether he would ever call me back at all.

The next morning, I met Stevan in the hallway and greeted him with a smile and a cough. After breakfast, he left for a full day in court and I sunk into the couch amid a sea of blankets, the TV remote, and Henry. I fell into a dreamy sleep that made the agony of my respiratory illness disappear. I was dreaming about a tropical paradise when the phone rang. I saw my doctor's telephone number come up on the TV screen. OMG – he's calling me back. He's really calling me back! I jumped up and turned to rush towards the phone when my foot got caught in one of the blankets. At this point, the world was moving in slow motion. My exhaustion claimed victory over my fight-or-flight response, I spun around and down I went, as if in a drunken blackout.

As I landed I felt a surge of electricity in my left shoulder. It was unlike any sensation I had ever experienced before. It took a few seconds for my eyes to reopen and the first thing that came into sight was Henry -- with my slipper in his mouth, tail wagging – waiting for me to play his favorite game, chase-me-and-try-to-get-back-what-I've-just-stolen-from-you. We play it all the time. Today would not be one of those days.

I couldn't lift my left arm, but I had to get the phone. I don't know how I picked my body off the floor, but I managed to lift the receiver in time. I recognized the voice: the receptionist from hell. What was I going to say to her right now? I told her what just happened and she told me to call 911 and get to the emergency room. Then she just hung up. I didn't get to tell her about my bronchitis and I didn't get to make an appointment with my doctor.

X-rays confirmed a fractured shoulder in two places. I accepted the painkillers the cute male nurse gave me, called a friend to come pick me up, and returned home to process what had just happened and what it meant for the rest of my week. With no idea how this unfortunate accident would impact the rest of my life, I sunk back down into the couch, pulled up my thick wool blankets, closed my eyes, and fell asleep – hoping for the tropical paradise dream to return.

The following days and weeks were filled with learning how to function with only one arm. Showering, cooking, writing, and housecleaning became unexpected challenges. Washing and drying my long hair was impossible, and Stevan became my reluctant hairdresser. He was as loving and supportive as he could be, but I'd glimpse him in the mirror rolling his eyes and making weird movements with his mouth that were definitely not in the smile category. I kept reassuring him (and myself) that this would be a memory in a few weeks and we'll have a good laugh about it all.

I canceled all of my yoga contracts and classes. I wrote a lot of refund checks and sealed the envelopes with one hand – tricky. After they were mailed out and corporate contracts canceled, I wondered how I'd be able to start over again once my shoulder healed. That was about to become the least of my worries.

Little did I know that after one week in, I'd be greeted by a sensation that was about to intensify this entire aggrieving experience. What was this weird, intense pain shooting from my neck down both of my arms? The investigation into this new affliction began, but answers eluded me. I called my doctors and each one sent me to another specialist who then sent me to someone else. One neurosurgeon told me to go home and just live with it. Really?

Days and weeks passed and the pain was unrelenting. I started on painkillers and even they did not stop this physical agony. I hated taking them and skipped some doses because all they did was make me sleepy. I spent most of my days on the couch with a heating pad draped over my shoulders, trying to breathe deeply and not cry out and scream. I spent all of my days with Henry by my side. He was aware that something was terribly wrong. My weight went from a healthy 134 to 109 pounds and I began to look as sick as I felt. I tried acupuncture. I tried Reiki. Even hypnosis. I bought a far-infrared sauna and did my meditations in this hot-box while tears streamed down my face. I wondered if I would ever be out of pain.

Friends and family were worried. Stevan later told me that he was scared to come home because he didn't know how he would find me, or if he would even find me alive. I'm ashamed to admit that those dark thoughts actually crossed my mind. I had spiraled into a deep depression. I was advised to go on anti-depressants. I took one pill, got dizzy, and went on an online forum for advice. There, thousands of people warned me that once on these drugs, the body will never want you to stop. I was terrified.

Even so, I knew that these medications help millions of people, but my inner knowing was clear: this route was not for me. I decided to give another holistic doctor a try. By now, I had a large paper accordion folder filled with patient notes and receipts from dozens of physicians, osteopaths, naturopaths, surgeons, and other specialists. It was totally full and should have represented a lifetime of medical care, but it was just twenty weeks. I sat in the cold examination room, alone, waiting, crying. The physician came in and listened, then went through the all too familiar medical routine. His recommendation was to have a nerve conduction test. Finally. Here was a suggestion that made sense to me. Could this be a way out of the pain? I made an appointment the next day.

A nerve conduction test consists of a series of needles in different areas to determine nerve damage and inflammation. It isn't a pleasant experience, and yet I sat still, breathed slowly, and tried to trust. Then, towards the end of the test, I had trouble breathing and got worried. What was wrong now? The doctor had punctured my lung. You can't make this stuff up. The doctor administering a test to try to get me out of excruciating pain had just punctured my lung. Back to the hospital I went.

Deep breathing was the one thing I could count on to slow me down, to calm my nervous system, and to find a modicum of balance in the hurricane that had become my life. Now even that was painful.

All I had left during the day was my beautiful yellow Lab, Henry. His love was ever present. He stayed with me. When I was ugly from crying, he didn't walk away; he came closer and cuddled up with me. Oh, how I loved this boy! I would look at him and cringe at the thought that someone so loving might ever have to suffer as I was. I could not stand the thought of his suffering. That image would haunt me and I wasn't sure why. Imagining Henry in pain was too much for me to bear. I took all of the love he was willing to give me. I soaked it all in and gave back all I could to this beautiful, sentient being whose purpose became saving me while I sought the help I needed to get my life back.

Determined to climb out of this abyss, I accepted a referral to a psychotherapist. A few sessions in, I knew this woman was really getting me. She was compassionate, intuitive, and intent on helping me. I was very clear about how I wanted to make the journey back. She emphasized spirituality and that resonated with me. I knew I was on the right path: psychotherapy, physical therapy, trigger point therapy, meditation, and soon, pain management therapy.

With a diagnosis of severe cervical radiculopathy, my first visit to the pain management doctor was terrifying. It was a waiting room filled with despair.

When I was called in, the doctor told me he would be giving me a shot in my spine that would hopefully relieve the pain. Stevan brought me in for my first shot and I was crying and shaking like a frightened infant. I was in so much pain already, I was scared that a shot in my spine would compound the pain. I didn't think I could stand any more pain.

As I undressed and slipped into a hospital gown, I glanced over at Stevan and saw his distress and sadness. At that moment I didn't know which of us I felt sorrier for. We were both so weary. The nurse escorted me into the treatment room and I lay face down on the table. The doctor explained what was about to happen, but his words sounded as if they were echoing off in the distance. There was a monitor visually tracking the details of my spine to help him navigate. There would be no guarantee that the injection would reach the exact place where the nerve was compressed, but the screen would help him get as close as possible. I was so weak and frightened. I just wanted to curl up and be held, rocked, and soothed. The room was cold. My tears were warm. A little pinch, a little burning, and it was over. Nothing more to do other than to go home and see if it took.

I literally watched the clock because I was told that the shot should kick in within 48 hours. I went to bed praying for something good to happen. And in 48 hours, it did. I was no longer writhing in pain. I wasn't in agony. It felt strange and wonderful. It was as if the heavens had opened up and a choir of angels were harmonizing, accompanied by a gigantic organ, and the music was just for me. I visualized myself practicing yoga again, walking in the sunshine. I moved slowly and cautiously, working to get my strength back. The days seemed brighter and for three glorious weeks, I was in a state of pure gratitude.

Until the pain came back. My mind fought it as hard as my body did, but agony knocked on the door and let itself back in.

All in all, it took three shots over a three-month period to get some ongoing pain cessation. Any relief felt like the angels singing in that beautiful choir. Slowly, slowly, the therapies were beginning to take. My amazing and insanely patient physical therapist was helping me get a little stronger; my trigger point therapist was giving me hours of relief unpacking those horrid trigger points and moving the fascia and scar tissue. My psychotherapist was teaching me to have faith, to trust that my body would heal. Dear friends were calling regularly to offer love and hope. And Stevan and Henry were by my side loving me. Just loving me.

I felt so much compassion for all who were suffering, those I knew and those I would never know. I realized then that most of us think about suffering only when it is our own. This experience forced me to transcend the limits of my compassion. I wasn't sure how, but I felt myself evolving. I even caught myself smiling, something I hadn't done in many months.

Here were the glimmers of light I'd been searching for in the dark, connecting me, completing me, healing me. How else can we truly connect to the core of who we are unless we are literally shaken to the core? We're layered so thickly with emotional armor, harboring our permission to disregard and dismiss what we'd otherwise disdain and defy. It is suffering, this shaking to the core, that affords us that glimpse into authentic compassion. Extreme suffering broke me open from deep within and I truly understood that I could no longer ignore the suffering of others. That was my beginning.

For two years I thought I wanted my old life back, but I was changed, and mine would be a different life now. I had a new sense of compassion inside me and although I didn't know where it would take me, I was ready to go.

5

KNOWLEDGE BY INTERNET

It's not what you look at that matters — it's what you see.

— HENRY DAVID THOREAU

My body was free from the constant, excruciating pain, but I'd still need a lot of healing to get my strength back, to gain weight, to feel less frightened. I wasn't ready to blast out of the house and start CrossFit, or go back to teaching, or do much of anything that required me to be vertical for any length of time. These two years had taken a toll and I'd have to move slowly towards my new normal. The activities that kept me occupied during my days were jewelry making and exploring the Internet.

Yoga-inspired jewelry design became a way to stay connected to the yoga community and to my practice. I called it "Hip & Holy Bling." The creative process was meditative and relaxing, each foray into it resulted in a lovely piece of jewelry made from gemstones, each with its own healing property and spiritual meaning. For an hour or two in my makeshift studio, I forgot about my troubles and focused on beauty and breath.

And on the Internet I could research anything I could think of. There was so much happening inside this cerebral cortex of mine. A lot of my research was about my health, but sometimes I would go on Facebook and scroll for hours -- the ultimate time drain and distraction we've come to love and despise. At that time, posts would just pop up and, videos would play spontaneously, whether you wanted them to or not.

One day, while wasting a few hours online, a video popped up on the screen. I brought my face a little closer because I wasn't exactly sure what I was seeing. It was the inside of a slaughterhouse filled with chickens. A huge motorized contraption was spinning in a circular motion, swooping up the chickens and killing them en masse. I looked on in horror and actually said aloud -- with no one to hear me except Henry -- "What the hell is this?"

I had never seen anything like it and I felt the

strangest sensation in my body. My brain was buzzing and trying to comprehend whether or not this was real, and if it was, why didn't I know about it and why was I so horrified? Actually, what was taking place inside me was a synaptic event: *I was making a connection*. For that moment, I was disoriented and very uncomfortable. A lifetime of miseducation had created an incalculable number of closed doors inside me, and those doors were about to be kicked open, one by one.

Instead of scrolling past that moving image, my eyes remained affixed while my brain put the pieces together. This is what happens between the farm to the fridge, isn't it? I shook my head as if it were an Etch-a-Sketch and I was trying to erase these images and start all over, but it was too late.

There was no un-seeing what I just saw and I suddenly felt compelled to know what else I didn't know. What else was I insensible to? Where have I been so wrapped up in my own life and its mysteries that I just did not see? It was an insatiable curiosity that propelled me to look further, to know more.

Googling "Animal Agriculture" is the epitome of higher education. I was not prepared for the snippets of information presented, articulated, and repeated in moving pictures and text. Baby piglets get castrated without anesthesia...Male chicks ground up in a macerator immediately after hatching because the egg industry can't use the boys...Cows impregnated only to keep them lactating, and babies ripped away from their crying mothers. What? What is this? What sick sci fi channel have I happened onto? But this was no fiction.

In an ever-flowing stream, this incredible information traveled from the unknown into the known. It entered my consciousness at an alarming speed. I was thirsty for more and drank from that well day in and day out. I watched documentaries. I read scientific studies, and agricultural journals, and I devoured spiritual books, too, the ones reiterating that there is no power greater than lovingkindness. Every now and then, when I felt up to it, I'd pack up the car and head for a sanctuary for animals rescued from the food system. There are several in New York State and neighboring New Jersey. At each one I visited, I got to know the residents as individuals, individuals who happened to be pigs or goats or turkeys.

All the adventuring, whether on the road or at my desk, brought me back to the same notions repeating in a loop inside my mind. Animals are suffering, animals who could just as easily be my beloved Henry. They are feeling pain. I know what pain feels like. I can't be part of that any longer. I won't be part of that any longer. How do I go vegan?

I'd been a teacher, and now I would become the student, knowing and learning simultaneously. I

studied all I could and absorbed. The health information alone was mind-blowing. The medical community, for all its advances, had largely gotten it wrong
on chronic disease, the "diseases of civilization." It all
started to make sense. Foods from the plant kingdom
are incredible medicine, and if I had just clicked my
heels three times, I might have known that this was
available all along.

There were so many vegan cookbooks to discover
and I found foods from the earth to be naturally deli-
cious. I was exhilarated and overjoyed by the journey
I was about to take. The Japanese poet Kenji
Miyazawa once avowed, "We must embrace pain and
burn it as fuel for our journey." My pain had a
purpose after all.

And all roads led to veganism after that.

Trips to the grocery store became adventures in
self-restraint, disbelief, and discovery. I wasn't the
same shopper I was a few months ago. I saw with
new eyes. When I watched someone shoving five or
six packages of chicken wings into their cart, no
doubt for some NFL happy hour, I saw the chickens
being mercilessly devoured in that killing machine.
The gallons of milk everyone seemed to be
purchasing were reminders to me that dairy has a
direct correlation to breast and prostate cancer, not to
mention that we're not baby calves and that milk was
not produced for us.

I needed only to look down at my own shoes to know that someone had died for my footwear. I walked to my closet in those shoes and saw abused animals everywhere I looked: sheep in my wool sweaters, silkworms in my silk blouses, cows in my belts and purses, and ducks painfully plucked for the down in my coats, unless it happened to have come from a duck or goose slaughtered for meat, making the feathers a "byproduct." They had suffered and were now buried just off the master bedroom. My closet was their graveyard. They were always there, but I never saw them.

I had never seen the laboratories where my shampoos, deodorants, toothpaste, make-up, and medicines were tested. But now, all I could see were restrained young animals being poked, prodded, and poisoned. And all I wanted to know was how I could have lived for five decades and been so blindly unaware.

A myriad of information and emotions were burning inside me. This was a flame that would burn for the rest of my days, and I knew it. I was okay with that. I was awake.

6

STEVAN

The goal in marriage is not to think alike, but to think together.

— Robert C. Dodds

We take our inner journeys alone. Not even those closest to us can ever really enter that soul cave where our deepest thoughts and emotions dwell: our pasts, our perceptions, our struggles, our fears, our deepest dreams. We travel that road alone and get to our destinations on our own time. Still, we share our lives with other humans and find love, comfort, strength, and companionship in their company. Ideally, marriage allows us to grow and change, whether we travel the exact same path as our partner or not. And sometimes, there's a snag.

By this time, my veganism was rock solid – no going back. There was no unseeing what I had seen, no un-learning what I now knew. I was happy and secure in my decision to live this way. Stevan, however, was not. He was not ready to give up what seemed like everything he was used to. He's a routine kind of guy. He liked what he liked when he liked it and wasn't interested in making a big lifestyle transition. I understood that. Sort of.

I still shopped for our food and cooked all the meals. I would still take a ticket at the deli counter and order a quarter pound of sliced turkey or roast beef for his lunch sandwiches. I would put the groceries away and the next day I would take out the meat to make his sandwich. Each time, I noticed myself frowning and swallowing hard. Something in my chest would get heavy. Treating this result of suffering and slaughter as if it was just something to eat went against every impulse of my conscience. I could feel the wrinkles on my face the grimaces were forming. I had to breathe more deeply.

One night I told him I would try to make the sandwiches, but I just could not stand in line and buy the deli meats any longer. It made me feel embarrassed, hurt, and like a hypocrite. He agreed to shop for his own lunches and I thanked him for that. Even after the hardship of shopping for animal products was gone, making the sandwiches was still too much. I seethed about it during the day and I brought it up when Stevan came home from work. We were at an impasse. He knew in his heart that I couldn't be flexible about this. I'm one to pick my battles carefully. This was the battle I chose to fight.

One night at dinner, we were having a conversation about veganism and animals in the food system. I spoke. He listened. He was probably rolling his eyes, but not so much that I could see. I knew he was sick of hearing these facts. I knew he was tired of my constant despair over the suffering. I knew it, but I couldn't stop. He's my person, the closest human to me. He needed to know what I now knew. I felt compelled to make him see.

He agreed one Saturday afternoon to watch the documentary, *Peaceable Kingdom*: The Journey Home, with me. It's about small farmers who believed they were doing animal agriculture the "right" way, but who eventually came to see that there was no right way. Despite the financial hardships and life upheavals that resulted, they got out of the business of raising animals for people to eat. I knew the film touched him. I saw him wipe a tear from his eye. He had seen me delve into activism -- going to protests, posting online, speaking to everyone we knew – and now he listened. I talked about the lives and deaths of the pigs and the chickens and the cows and the fishes. And then he looked up at me with those loving brown eyes and said, "But you know I love animals."

My fist hit the table with a loud bang. The dinner plates bounced. I can only imagine the rage on my face. With all the calmness I could muster (which wasn't nearly enough) I replied, "You don't love animals; you love dogs. You love our dog. You can't love the animals you let be ripped apart and brutally slaughtered. You can't love animals you eat. You literally eat them. How the hell can you sit there and say you love them?" Silence.

A tension-filled ten days went by. I didn't make his lunch. He didn't ask me to. Dinners were vegan – take it or leave it. My heart, my soul, and every cell of my body were not messing around. I had been to the mountain and had seen the truth. I could no longer countenance lies or excuses.

I vividly remember the words Stevan spoke to me on day 11. I will always remember them, because as Maya Angelou told the world: "They may forget what you said, but they will never forget how you made them feel." I felt complete when Stevan said, "I've decided to go vegan. I love you, but I'm not doing this for you. I'm doing this because it's the right thing to do." Cue the just-got-to-heaven music with the angelic choir singing.

We could now live this compassionate life together. I would not have to see, shop for, touch, cook, or serve another dead animal, or piece of an animal, or secretion of an animal that would lead to slaughter in the end. Not ever. My husband the divorce lawyer got it. He made the connection. Oh, happy day! He did this for his love of the animals and, perhaps more than he was willing to admit, his love for me. And for that, I will always be grateful.

7

AVANI

When the suffering of another causes you to feel
pain, do not submit to the initial desire to flee from
the suffering, but on the contrary, come closer, as
close as you can, and try to help.

— LEO TOLSTOY, *A CALENDAR OF WISDOM*

Country roads exude the sense of peace and calm of a bygone era we'll probably never get back again. The roads near my home make me feel that way often. One in particular is called Freedom Road. It has a sharp curve, with a diamond-shaped black and white sign reading 10 miles per hour for a reason. If you don't slow down at that curve, you're likely to careen into the corn field or even an oncoming car.

When I'd turn the bend at my compliant ten miles an hour, I'd always notice the tall silver silo of the dairy farm coming up on the left. I was mesmerized by the endless green fields, the big, red barn with peeling white shutters, and the rolling fences that framed the entire bucolic scene.

Just a few yards away from the road in front of the barn stood three metal and wooden crates, larger than dog crates, but not much. I'd never really noticed them before, but driving by this particular day, I saw three calves, each in their own crate, right on the side of the road. I could tell they were babies. Two were light brown and speckled; the other was all dark. I slowed down my car as if being drawn by a magnet. I drove off the road, onto the dirt, and into the farm.

This would not have happened years ago. I would have driven right by this farm with visions of sweet cows grazing in the pasture and I would have thought those babies were just so cute. It would have never occurred to me that these animals might be suffering or that I had any ability to help them. But the shadowed obscurity of truth was in my rearview mirror. I was seeing this for what it was. And it wasn't adorable at all. I had reached another plateau in my paradigm shift – the one that would propel me to action.

I approached the dark calf and began to swat the flies away from her warm body. It was a hot summer day and there was no water or food in the crate. She was tethered to it with a coarse rope tied tightly around her neck, as were the other two calves. The ropes forbade them to move more than a few feet in any direction. The ropes were tangled and weaved from their necks and under their legs, making any movement difficult. This calf was filthy and panting and clearly terrified. My heart was racing and breaking at the same time.

I got a bottle of water from my car and poured some into my cupped hands for her to drink. She took it, but I believe she was hoping it was her mother's milk, milk she'd never get to taste. I went from one calf to another, trying to bring some pittance of affection, some water and a distraction from a pathetic and purposeless existence. These were babies crying for their mothers -- mothers who were inside that big red barn, crying for their newborns, as the milk meant for them was pumped through metal contraptions hooked up to their udders, into a giant vat in another room in the barn.

I stayed for an hour. The sun was going down. Before I left, the dark calf looked at me intensely. It was a look that can only be felt, and not described, not even in the most eloquent of prose. She looked into me and through me and touched a part of me that I had yet to discover. I went home with warm tears running down my face. I dropped to the floor, hugged

Henry tightly, and cried some more. I slept, and dreamt of going back to that farm in the middle of the night, cutting those tight ropes, taking those calves, and never looking back.

I did go back, but not to take the calves and run. I went back a few times a week to bring them food, water, and love. I called the dark calf "my sweet girl" and that's who she became. If I had treats in my pocket, she'd nuzzle me to try to get them out. She would eat from my hand and let me clean her up and sing to her, as she'd come closer for a cuddle. Mine was the only human kindness she'd ever known. I visited with all of the calves, but there was something special between my sweet girl and me.

The little male calf in the crate next to hers was feisty and angry, rightfully so, and it took several tries to get near him. I felt such a sense of victory when he finally allowed me to feed him apples. He'd take the apple, but wasn't interested in any further interaction. I could tell he just wanted out. He'd kick and run, only to be pulled back by a quick choke of his rope collar. The other female calf didn't want anything to do with me. She'd take some snacks now and then, but would always retreat back inside her crate. I had a special bond with one calf, but I was fascinated by them all, by how different they were, how unique and exceptional was each personality.

About ten days later when I pulled up to the farm,

I noticed that one crate was empty. The feisty male calf had been taken away, sold to slaughter for veal. The void made me gasp. The emptiness that day was overwhelming. My heart was broken. And then there were two.

I met the farmer, a sturdy, friendly man with a broad smile and missing teeth. His was a fourth-generation dairy farm and this work was all he'd ever known. He allowed me to visit the calves and fill up buckets of water from his utility room off of the main barn where the cows were milked. He tolerated my questions, even suggestions to turn his dairy farm into an animal sanctuary. Mostly, he laughed at me. When I asked him where the boy calf went, he gave me that look as if to say, "You know what happened to that calf, and I know you know." He engaged in conversation, but I felt he'd prefer I didn't come around. I was an annoyance, like the flies on the calves' faces. But even more, I was a reminder of that spark of compassion he had to unconsciously struggle to keep down in order to continue to "raise" these animals the way he did.

I wanted to visit often, so sometimes I'd come bearing gifts. I brought him and his farmhand vegan ice cream made from cashews or coconuts. Once I brought the farmer a gallon of almond milk and a sleeve of Oreo cookies. He graciously accepted my gifts, and he paid back with full access to the farm. I got to hang out with the mama cows in the barn and watch them parade out to the fields, a small privilege not afforded dairy cows on the larger "factory" farms where most milk comes from. I wondered why these didn't just run away and never come back, but their food was in the barn, and maybe they held the hope of reuniting with their babies in that big barn, too.

All I could see, when they were herded back in hours later, were slaves. Their heads were locked into metal gates. They were standing on cement floors with thin rubber mats under their hoofs. And their sensitive utters were clamped with metal and tubing. They could not roam free – they couldn't move at all. They were being exploited for the milk they'd produced for their babies. It no longer looked natural, bucolic, or peaceful as it once had. It looked more like hell.

It was September and the summer was coming to an end. I'd been visiting this farm for almost three months now, and my sweet girl was getting bigger. She was outgrowing her crate. She had been in the same spot every single day since I first saw her. Day in and day out, in the extreme heat and the summer downpours, she had not walked more than a few feet from that grimy crate. I asked the farmer if we could take her for a walk, just to let her move around, but he never took my request seriously.

I felt a sense of desperation when I'd think of her

sedentary, motionless, and lonely life. And I felt terror knowing what lay ahead for her: artificial insemination on the device coined by the industry as a "rape rack." Nine months carrying her baby and being milked through pregnancy. Having that baby taken from her soon after giving birth. Grieving and wailing for her baby. Returning to her job as a milk slave inside the barn. And eventually when her milk runs out, she'll go to slaughter like her sons, not for prime beef but hamburger or pet food and, certainly, leather. How could I let this happen? I couldn't.

A few days later I drove by the farm and waited until I saw the farmer's green pick-up truck. I pulled in and started my friendly banter with him. He knew how I felt about this calf by now, and it was probably a source of dull amusement for him. But today, I would ask him if I could have this calf and take her to sanctuary. He saw the seriousness in my face. He wasn't answering me, so I paused for a few seconds and asked him again. It was when I offered to pay him for the calf that he finally agreed. He wasn't going to release her out of the goodness of his heart. To him, this was merely a business transaction and a way to get rid of me. But she was going to be free and all I could think about is the massive misery she'd be spared.

On the day of the rescue, I asked him to show me which cow inside the barn was my sweet girl's mother. He sneered at me, a now familiar look, and walked me towards a large cow in one of the stalls inside the barn. She was hooked up to the equipment attached to her utters and her head was centered within the metal bars that surrounded it. I looked at her and could not contain my tears. I told her that her baby girl was going to live a different life, a life of freedom. I told her that her baby would be taken care of and loved, and that I was so sorry they could not live together as a family. She looked directly at me as I asked simultaneously for her understanding and her forgiveness. I touched her soft head and turned to go outside to help with the rescue.

When the rope around the little calf's neck was cut and she was put on the truck that would take her – literally – down Freedom Road, I fell to my knees and wept. This was early October. When she arrived at the sanctuary in Ohio, she was welcomed with love. They named her Avani, which means "Earth" in Sanskrit. The sanctuary owners sent me pictures of Avani running and playing in the field with the other bovines, jumping near the barns with the sheep, eating from fresh bales of hay, and quietly resting beneath a tree. My sweet girl was free. My heart was sated. The tears I cried were of joy for her and sorrow for all the others.

8

FAMILY AND FRIENDS: EXIT STAGE LEFT

When she transformed into a butterfly, the caterpillars spoke not of her beauty, but of her weirdness. They wanted her to change back into what she always had been. But she had wings.

— DEAN JACKSON

I continued to live and learn the vegan life, and experience the ongoing awakening that had, quietly and seamlessly, restructured my being. Every cell in my body knew with certainty the myriad ways in which living a vegan life could heal the body and the spirit. Every single cell.

I realized that this was the way for me to live in harmony with nature, and that phrase, "the way it's always been," was nothing more than familiarity diverting us from the process of evolution. I tried to rationalize and understand the decades I'd lived without giving this a single thought. I agonized over not discovering all this sooner. The only explanation I could come up with was that we are all indoctrinated, led from an early age to swallow a host of notions, for reasons other than the good of all. It became clear that corporate interests – Big Ag, Big Food, Big Pharma – aided and abetted by government, allow profits to override ethics.

I also learned that keeping animals off our plates could lead to substantial health benefits, and that the inefficient business of raising animals for food was polluting our waterways, destroying the rain forests, and making a massive contribution to climate change. I was furious and I was frustrated. The veil had been lifted. I saw the insanity and the injustice -- and this big reveal created a tsunami of feelings that would be tough to navigate for a long, long time.

The ghosts in the grocery store haunted me with each shopping trip. Everyone seemed to have a piece of a plastic-wrapped animal in their carts, and the madness of their nonchalance was overwhelming. The disconnect was everywhere and my only escape was to linger in the produce aisle until I could calm down. I wanted to approach everyone. I wanted to tell them what I had discovered. I was sure they'd want to know what their choices were doing to other beings.

And if they didn't care about that, I could enlighten them about the effects on their own bodies of animal foods, with their abundance of cholesterol and saturated fat and their dearth of fiber.

Climate change could be a conversation starter, too. I'd try to make eye contact, but more often than not, I would quickly feel like the stranger I obviously was. They didn't know me. They didn't know that my intention was not to guilt them, shame them, or shock them. I just wanted to share the truth, so it could live somewhere other than inside me. When I did manage to say something, I could see it in their eyes: they not only thought of me as a stranger; they thought I was just plain strange.

But my loved ones, I'd have to save *them*, because I loved them and they loved me and they'd undoubtedly want to know. They would be eager to understand why I'd made such a huge life shift. I'd appeal to their compassion, to their intellect, and to their desire to do the right thing. They would sense how much I cared about them and how this information could transform them, too. I was sure they would be open to the volumes of evidence: both the scientific studies on the health benefits of a plant-based diet, and the eye-opening investigations and undercover videos of the hideous ways in which humans treat animals so that we can consume meat, eggs, and dairy products. They would come to understand that all the foods they felt they'd be giving up, didn't belong in us in the first place. They would thank me and ask me to help them with their transition. We would bond over compassion and recipes.

And then I woke up. That never happened and I was bewildered as I stepped into this new reality. Sharing this epiphany became the only way to remain sane. Stevan came to understand it. He had listened, then watched film *Peaceable Kingdom*: The Journey Home, and soon after made the connection. But he lived with me. He slept with me. He was legally obligated to listen. My impassioned pleas fell on deaf ears with the rest of the family and most of my friends.

My son is a classically trained chef and although he'd never turn away from a good debate, discussion of this subject devolved into an argument every time. My mother-in-law called me a "fanatic," and my friend David called me "one note," because I spoke about veganism a lot. Okay, I spoke about veganism all the time. A discovery this important needs to be shared -- shouted from the proverbial rooftops and noted in Facebook posts.

But the discomfort of this topic changed the dynamic of the conversation with almost everyone. I could pinpoint the very second that I lost them. No one wanted to delve into these ideas, and if I'd bring them up, the shift in energy was as sharp as a sudden hailstorm on a bright summer day. My choice became obvious. I'd have to quell any feelings, thoughts, or discussion around being vegan if I wanted to have a relationship with just about everyone I knew. I'd take little dainty steps on the eggshells they placed at my feet. I'd try to tread oh, so carefully. I failed at that too. It was becoming an exhausting way to live -- and love.

There were several couples we'd gone out to dinner with for years. They loved to drink and laugh and talk about what they'd been up to, the latest in sports or gossip; and sometimes the wives would talk with the wives and the husbands with the husbands. When I brought up our new lifestyle, the energy shift got real with them, too. They would ask a few questions when Stevan and I ordered our "special" meals, but they must not have liked the answers because they stopped calling to make plans. We had become the mirror held up to their conscience and they wanted no part of it. Our social circle was getting smaller and we'd have to adapt. I began to make dinners at home and invite friends over. This seemed to work well with a few. Others made their way out of our lives.

Conversations that were once innocuous and inoffensive suddenly became swords made from words. "We attended the horse races at Saratoga…We had a fabulous vacation at Sea World…My God, this corned beef sandwich is to die for… I got an amazing deal on a genuine leather handbag…." Phrases I could have said a year ago now stung my ears and pierced my heart. The person uttering these words meant no harm to me, but I knew the harsh reality behind the words and they did not. That's excusable. But they didn't want to know, and that hurt me the most. They wouldn't let me explain, yet I was desperate to explain. Little can devastate a sensitive soul more than living among loved ones who can't understand, or won't.

It began to feel as if I was living in a dream I had one night, in which I was being held in a prison. It was massive and dark and frightening. Everyone I knew was there with me, each in our own horrid cell. One night, a key appeared out of nowhere. I picked it up and tried the lock on my cell door. It opened. I'd been inside that cell for so long, I wasn't even sure what I should do. But freedom is like a magnet, so I opened the cell door and escaped.

I looked around and everyone else's door was still locked. I walked over to another cell and tried my key in the lock. Lo and behold, that cell door opened, as well! And the next, and the next. I opened as many cell doors as I could, running from one to another, my heart racing. When I reached the last cell in the row, I turned back to see everyone still inside their open cells.

I didn't understand. Why were they just sitting

there, staying in the cell confining them, imprisoning them? I screamed, "Come out! I'm letting you out. I've found a way out." But only a few would even move towards the cell door, curious to see what was waiting outside that captivity, that darkness. They chose to stay. They had been there so long the cell felt like home. I could not convince them to come outside with me. I would have to leave them there. I started to run, faster and faster, running to get out of there. The dream shook me awake.

Which is the dream? Which is real life? I couldn't distinguish. I missed my family. I didn't know them anymore, and they absolutely didn't know me. I was struggling to find the balance that could allow me to accept them and feel heard and understood at the same time. But I couldn't find the key that would unlock their hearts and open their minds to want to know what I so wanted to share with them, to share with love.

9

THE COMMITMENT

We can easily forgive a child who is afraid of the dark; the real tragedy of life is when men are afraid of the light.

— PLATO

E dgar Kupfer was a survivor of the Dachau death camp. After his liberation, he furtively scrawled the following message on the wall of his hospital barrack: "I refuse to eat animals because I cannot nourish myself by the sufferings and by the death of other creatures. I refuse to do so, because I suffered so painfully myself that I can feel the pain of others by recalling my own sufferings."

Although the worst day of my life cannot compare

with that of someone who experienced the Holocaust, I can feel the pain of others by recalling my own suffering. This is the empath's mantra, and one that has both served me well, and haunted me, for most of my life.

If a friend would call to unload her misery, I'd voluntarily absorb it and it would stay with me, even after the friend had forgotten her angst. I kept it on hold for her, like a sweater on layaway at her favorite department store. Her despondency was safe with me -- inside me, gnawing at my emotions. I'd wrack my brain trying to come up with ways to help my friend, solve her problem, ease her pain, protect her heart -- all the while sacrificing my own equilibrium and whatever peace I was enjoying before our conversation. My sister and I used to call this "the peanut butter sandwich syndrome." I would be agonizing about someone else's pain, while they had already moved on and were eating a peanut butter sandwich, as if nothing at all had happened.

Once you've seen the unfathomable suffering the animals endure, it is hard to get it out of your mind, especially if you're an empath. It's no wonder that most people I spoke to refused to let me show them pictures or tell them stories. It's quite a feat to witness how far we will go to make life hell for other living beings, as well as for ourselves. Just when I thought I'd seen everything -- every gadget of animal torture, confinement, branding, mutilation, restriction, and slaughter -- a new one would come into my view. I would shake my head no until my neck ached, wondering who stayed up at night concocting this evil. I would stay up at night myself, wondering how unfamiliar I'd been with the ways of the world in which I'd grown up and matured and should know well by now. Each new piece of information was unimaginable, yet it was real.

As I'd recall the pain I suffered every hour of every day for almost 24 months, I realized that the pain for these animals only stops in death. This was soul-crushing for me, and the fact that I had no control to stop the madness, haunted me. It still does.

When Thanksgiving came around on my second year of being vegan, I went to the family gathering, wanting to be part of the holiday symphony during our one big yearly meal together. This was the one dinner which we'd gather round and admire before devouring the feast and counting our blessings in between the cranberry sauce and the football game.

But this year would be different – a turning point. The previous Thanksgiving, I'd drunk massive amounts of alcohol to mask my vegan feelings, and to go along with tradition and be with my family. I ate my plant-based meal in a quiet, inebriate state at the far end of the table. It worked okay, except for the killer hangover I endured the next day. As I sat down at this year's table, still too sober to block out the discomfort, I observed the people I loved, sitting around that crowded table, gnawing on a turkey's leg or cutting into a piece of a turkey's breast, drenched in gravy rich in drippings from that turkey's skin.

In the kitchen a few feet away sat the looming, threadbare carcass on the counter, stripped of nearly everything except his bones, or hers. These were the remains of a once-living being who had had no name, who was literally nothing to anyone, and who had likely known in life only suffering and pain. I stayed seated at the table, knowing that to help with the cleanup would mean having to witness the war-torn carcass in the kitchen. I wanted to run out the front door and, like Forrest Gump, just keep running.

Staring into Stevan's eyes, I at least found connection and a grounding sensation that kept me aware of my surroundings. In between bites and utensils clanging, I heard raucous laughter and overlapping conversations that created a mutant buzz. I felt that slow-motion wave of anxiety washing over me, shades of the China Rose so long ago. Words were muttered and muted. My presence at the table grew smaller and smaller until I felt that I'd disappeared. No one could see me, know what I was feeling, or that I was literally drowning in a sea of despair. If I were to chime in with the truth about the suffering that preceded this meal, it would surely be the demise of the happy family get-together. And some people had traveled so far. I poured another drink and played with Henry, who was lying at my feet.

When I got home, I threw up. Then I cried for an hour. I was drained and distraught. Sitting at that table, I'd felt like a total stranger among the very people I loved and who loved me. I couldn't put myself through that again. That was the day I made the commitment: To preserve my sanity and my emotional health, I would no longer sit with people who were gorging on the dead or exploited. If someone wanted to be with me, to eat with me, they'd need to refrain from consuming animals, fishes, dairy products, and eggs for that one hour. The other 8,759 hours in the year were their business. I thought that was a reasonable request. Others did not.

I took "The Liberation Pledge," which is simply a commitment to live vegan values and refuse to sit where animals' bodies are being eaten. I knew about the violence. I acknowledged it. I had watched animals begging for their lives, tortured as they were. I had seen the cruelty with my own eyes. I couldn't pretend that it was okay. I couldn't condone the suffering and I couldn't watch as people dismissed it.

It made me sad to think about not being with my family. I didn't expect they'd understand this vow, and they didn't. It made Stevan sad, as he would continue to go, partly out of a sense of obligation, but also love for his mom. He understood why I couldn't go. I understood why he had to.

The situation was awful. We had asked to have a vegan Thanksgiving – I would have been thrilled to host -- but that seemed to family members like no Thanksgiving all. There was no room for negotiation. Even though there was no upside to my decision, in terms of family relationships, it was liberating not to have to put myself through the contradiction of right and wrong action. The parameters were clear. I stood strong in my conviction and I protected my heart.

This commitment applied to lunch with friends, dinners out, and even coffee at Starbucks. Surprisingly, my real friends understood and happily obliged. It wasn't a hardship – they all enjoyed our meals together and some were curious to know more. It was a heavy load lifted and it was one way I could honor my emotions and the animals at the same time. This is a choice that not even most vegans make, but it was right for me.

10

FINDING MY WAY BACK OM

All beings tremble before violence. All fear death. All love life. See yourself in others. Then whom can you hurt? What harm can you do?

— BUDDHA

Yoga is a practice you keep coming back to. Not to perfect it -- that's why they call it a practice -- but to seek it out as a constant sanctuary of sorts. It's like prayer without religion, movement without the spandex and gym shoes. Putting on your own oxygen mask first. And to me, it's coming home.

I was lucky to have had the teacher training I did. It wasn't a weekend or even a month in Costa Rica. It was a rigorous yearlong training that demanded a deep dive into all that yoga is meant to be. I entered in thinking that yoga would keep me in good shape, make me calmer and more peaceful, and speak to the hippie I saw when I looked in the mirror. I didn't want to read about what my diet and lifestyle habits had to do with it. I fought against it and mocked it and ignored it. Until I didn't.

As I told you early on, that first book we had to read was called *Jivamukti Yoga*. Breaking it down, *jiva* refers to a living being, human or otherwise; *mukti* means liberation. Human liberation, animal liberation -- it all sounds good to me. But I didn't make the connection until I lived through the opposite of liberation.

During my illness and injury and through all the pain I couldn't wish away, I became a prisoner of my body and emotions. I was relegated to stillness and was forced to see and touch the suffering I had wanted to resist. When it was so close, I had no other option but to take it on, to feel it in myself and see it in others. I realized then that despite our differences, we all share the capacity to suffer – and to want to free ourselves from that suffering. That experience brought home the very essence of what yoga had been trying to teach me. It comes back with every *asana*, every meditation, every conscious breath. We are not separate. We are not separate. We are not separate.

Returning to yoga, my practice began to look and

feel different. Yoga is the work of the body and the soul, a practice of non-violence that can easily move into all aspects of life. Yoga creates a cease-fire between the ego and one's true nature. When I chanted *Lokah samastah sukhino bhavantu* – "May all beings be happy and free" -- at the end of a yoga practice, it started to mean something to me. We can chant the words, but if our actions don't contribute to that freedom, what's the point?

Ahimsa is another word often tossed around in the yoga community. It means non-harming, non-violence towards any living being. As the first limb of yoga, it is meant to be taken seriously as the most important tenet of the entire practice. I'd used it routinely in classes I taught, but hypocritically and without fully embracing either its necessity or its power. I taught it, but until now, I hadn't lived it. Now I was.

Yoga translates as "union," union with the Divine, with oneself, and with our fellow beings. We are not separate. Yoga taught me that. So did Henry and Avani and the animals at the sanctuaries. We are not separate. *Lokah samastah sukhino bhavantu.*

11

THE JOY AND SORROW OF SERVING
THIS MISSION

*Think about it: virtually every atrocity in the
history of humankind was enabled by people who
turned away from a reality that seemed too painful
to face, while virtually every revolution for peace
and justice has been made possible by a group of
people who chose to bear witness and demanded
that others bear witness as well.*

— MELANIE JOY PH.D., ED.M.

As I logged onto Facebook one morning,
coffee cup in hand, I steeled myself for the
information wars, beginning with this
message from an old high school acquaintance: "I am
married to a veterinarian and have the utmost respect
for what you portray. However; I find the pictures of

tortured animals on Facebook so upsetting that I feel I need to un-friend you. I just wanted you to understand why I am un-friending you. Good luck to you and your cause."

That's me, a woman with a cause -- and one less Facebook friend. Vegan activism, online and off, had become an exercise in radical acceptance. To me, this is more than a "cause," and no mere hobby. My colleagues in this movement are not a coterie of counter-culture types trying to be heard. Animal rights may well be the social justice issue of our time, and the vegan living it calls for also addresses other crucial problems: climate change, deforestation, species extinction, air and water pollution, soil erosion, and many human health concerns, certainly coronary heart disease, the number one killer of women and men in the developed world.

Trust me: I didn't choose to become an activist. When I internalized the conviction to live in a way that caused the least harm and did the most good possible, conforming to societal norms became more painful than the rejection of family and friends. I had to accept that people would un-friend me in countless ways. It's easier for some to reject a friendship, than accept the suffering caused by their own choices.

Those who became activists in the civil rights movement were met with violent resistance. They unveiled the cruelties of segregation through marches and peaceful protests until people across America were aware of the atrocities and important changes followed, although the job is far from finished. Those who opposed the civil rights movement, and the anti-slavery movement before it, had a vested interest in halting these efforts in their tracks. They chose to see the "other" and desperately wanted to keep their supremacy and opportunities for economic exploitation alive for as long as they could.

Women's rights activists struggled to get their grossly overdue right to vote in the 19th and early 20th centuries, and feminists continue to demand that the world see and destroy the gender inequality that still lingers. Gay rights activists marched and filed lawsuits and spoke out until their right to love and marry was acknowledged, and now it is the law of the land. And yet, the LGBTQ movement still labors for full justice and faces pushback from religious groups and frightened people who see them as "other."

American medical anthropologist and physician Paul Farmer said it best: "The idea that some lives matter less is the root of all that is wrong with the world." Animal liberation advocates agree whole-heartedly, and we expand the commitment to include all lives, human and nonhuman alike. We are up against the most powerful industries in the world – with unwavering funding and support from our own government. They see animals as commodities and nothing more. If the social justice movements fighting for our own species can take decades and centuries to effect change, the plight of the animals is that much more of a challenge. Yeah, we are the David to their Goliath, but we all know how that story ends. We may not live long enough to see it. Not going to stop us.

It can be excruciating to go through life – walk the aisles of the grocery store, watch TV, listen to conversations at work, turn the pages of a magazine, pass by a restaurant -- and be bombarded by the very cruelty you're working so hard to end. In the world as it is, however, these sights and sounds and products and preferences are legal and normal. They're even glorified, often amplified, and constantly justified. Recognizing cruelty and responding to it is an awakening that happens for some and not for others. And I scratch my head and wonder why some are liberated from indoctrination and others choose to remain enslaved.

For the ones who make the connection, however, there is a tribe of hearts: others who feel that same deep longing for more peace on this planet and less suffering for all beings. These are the ones who vow to devote the rest of their days to right a wrong. These outliers, while flawed humans like the rest of us, motivate, lift up, and support the mission. We offer hope to one another, validation that we are on the right side of history, and that justice will one day -- someday -- prevail.

With so many people in my life leaving, the void has been filled with fellow activists. There is joy in knowing how many of us there are and that our numbers are growing each day.

Again, I didn't choose to follow this path. I became a vessel for the message and couldn't stop if I wanted to. I never believed the idea before, that a life's calling can flow through you in an unstoppable stream, but I do now. I've trekked through the stages necessary to move through: shock, outrage, confusion, sorrow, compassion and finally, sheer determination.

The explosion of the vegan movement is a joyful experience and serves to balance the deep emotional toll that activism takes. The same capital that was once used to fund big agri-business is now being funneled into developing plant-based foods and materials to replace the use of animals. I smile every day when I read that someone is making leather from pineapples or eggs from mung beans. I am profoundly proud to be part of this caravan of peace. And, as the layers are peeled back, I find myself interested in having a gentler footprint overall, living a little greener, consuming a little less. I can also peer more deeply into other forms of oppression to which I'd been oblivious because of my personal privilege on the planet. This type of activism cracks the code of the heart and opens it up to include everyone. We are not separate. We are not separate.

Thinking about my sweet girl, Avani, and her life of freedom at the animal sanctuary brings enormous pleasure. The Talmud tells us that "He who saves one life, saves the entire world." If only. But when I stop and think about how I found her and where she is now, and all the suffering she was spared, and that I had a hand in that freedom -- well, I shed a tear now and then just thinking about her.

When I reflect on how my husband opened his heart to hear my message and then took the vegan plunge, well, that brings me joy, too, and it brought us even closer together as life partners. With every person I guide towards a vegan life as their coach, my heart rejoices. I'm so happy for them and I always give a little wink to the animals and silently say, "One less person who'll hurt you now."

I didn't respond to my high school friend's Facebook message for a few days. I wanted my response to be concise and clear, because it would be our last correspondence. When I was ready, I wrote back:

"I truly understand your reasons for un-friending me. You are not the first to do that. I know that you are married to a veterinarian. However, that does not automatically correlate with understanding animal activism or how profound this movement is. Actually,

veterinarians are the only professionals who eat their patients. I've had many discussions with my veterinarian about the fact that he may very well be a dog and cat lover, but it is impossible to be a true animal lover and not be vegan. You either love animals or you eat and wear animals; you simply can't do both.

Please understand that these pictures you are offended by are real and these atrocities happen to innocent animals every second of every day. Refusing to look doesn't make their suffering go away. Refusing to change perpetuates that suffering. Instead of being offended by the pictures, perhaps you might instead become offended by the cruelty and begin to live in accordance with your values of kindness and mercy. Personal choices are only personal when there are no victims.

I wish you good health, happiness, and a life of compassion."

I then returned to my Facebook page and posted the following, because I am a hopeless quotation junkie. It comes from Philip Wollen, former vice-president of Citibank and general manager at Citicorp in Australia. He walked away from his high profile, high finance career to become a philanthropist of kindness and an avid animal activist. His words convey precisely what I was feeling in my heart, and following my heart was the only path I could walk now:

"Activists live more intense, sensitive and observant lives than others. So, by definition, we are constantly vulnerable to the ubiquitous cruelty that exists. But, if forced to make a binary choice, I would rather burn out living a compassionate, authentic life than rust out living a cruel, unexamined life. For me, there are no regrets. There is no going back."

12

AN APOLOGY TO JASON

"The parenting journey holds the potential to be a spiritually regenerative experience for both the parent and the child, where every moment is a meeting of spirits. And both parent and child appreciate that each dances on a spiritual path that's unique — holding hands and yet alone."

— DR. SHEFALI TSABARY

When I reflect on the years I spent as a single parent, my mind often returns to a sense of deep regret for not knowing some important things sooner. Oh, the wisdom I'd have shared with my child, if only life was like the Cher song and I could *turn back time*. And so, I wrote this letter. It's a source of self-reflection, a purging of sorts, and a love letter -- a weaving together of yesterday's struggles with profound gratitude for what I've since learned and actualized.

Dear Jason –

In the summer of 1981, in the middle of a Tucson heatwave, I brought you into the world, unaware of the profound changes life would hold for us both. While pregnant, I remember being told not to go into the hot tub, because you would turn into a hard-boiled egg. I stopped drinking coffee, soda, alcohol, even wine. The artificial sweeteners went too. With the information available to me then, I knew I wanted to create the perfect surroundings for you, and I wanted you to be comfortable during the brief time you resided within me. I was the perfect Airbnb host.

I remember eating half of a watermelon every single day and a pint of ice cream every single night. It was probably the most self-indulgent time of my life and I loved every minute of it. Your crib and dressing table were deftly prepared in anticipation of your arrival. I smiled every day that I waited for you, knowing that my interpretation of love would never be the same.

I was only twenty-six and carried with me the undercurrent of all the traumas that had affected me and accompanied me throughout my short life. Was I ready for a child? Probably not, but having one was my greatest desire and you were my greatest gift.

The partnership that brought you into being didn't last very long, and you and I were on our own from the time you were less than a year old. There wasn't a cell in my body that wasn't sure of this love and I was determined to do the best I could to let you know, to give you the sense of "always gonna love you." I hope I've succeeded in, at least, doing that.

I was young, indoctrinated, and oblivious to so much that was going on around me. I suppose when you're young and focused on your own life and the responsibilities of caring for an infant, the realities of the world are not at the forefront of your awareness. As I look back, they certainly were not in mine. I was, as you are, a product of my upbringing and my conditioning. I was completely uninformed of what true health was. I rarely, if ever, thought about the environment and my footprint's being gentle or harsh. And for some reason that will haunt me forever, I didn't think about the other living beings on this planet as worthy of my attention or my compassion. It was humans all the way. Myself as a human, my friends, and – most of all -- you.

Without that elevated consciousness, I lived at a rather base level, although I thought I was much more evolved than most. How narcissistic I was! -- and disconnected. There was no one in my entire world to show me how to live in the light, so I remained in the dark and that's what I passed on to you, my beautiful son. I'm sorry I didn't know better sooner.

I believe that if things were different back then, you would have grown up with a healthier body and a clearer mind. We moved around a lot because I was still searching for myself while I grasped for a better life for us. I wanted to give you everything I could and never make you feel that you had less than anybody else. I sought out the smallest spaces in the best neighborhoods to make you feel part of a community. I made my space in the living room, so you could enjoy the sanctuary of a bedroom, but coupled with the selflessness, there was selfishness, too. I had an addiction to shopping that I hid beneath the fabricated illusions and excuses, 'Kids need so much stuff,' and "This will make me happy." The end result was more debt, and more struggle.

I know you would have preferred a different blueprint. I wish I could have given you the stable family life you deserved – I had no reference of that stability in my own life, and was unable to build that foundation for you. Having two parents in your life might have made you feel more secure. And perhaps some sisters or brothers would have given you the fun and support system you missed and most likely desired. I'm sorry I couldn't give you that. But hey -- you and I had some cool trips across the country and beyond. We weren't lacking for cultural and recreational activities. There was no shortage of love and laughter. We had what we had.

As I write these thoughts to you, I am grateful and elated that you have grown into a wonderful human being. You've accomplished a lot, and you overcame the obstacles in your way. You've earned degrees and training certificates, traveled the world, married, had two beautiful children, and teach all over the globe. You enjoy creativity, political debate, nature, and music. You're smart and kind and a very good father. You should be proud. I am proud of the man you are.

As I'm sure you know as a parent yourself, some children are similar in personality and temperament to their parents. You and I are not. We've had our quarrels, differences, and even a period of time where we didn't speak at all, but I believe our bond is unbreakable. We can see the light in each other, and that light will always guide us back.

By now you know the depth of love a child brings into your life. You understand the lengths you'll go to in order to protect them, guide them, and shelter them from harm. You lie awake wondering if you're doing the best you can for them. You want to be secure in yourself as a role model and as a provider and protector of their fragile, impressionable, beautiful souls. You want them to be happy and safe. I've wanted that for you every single day of your life. Be happy and safe.

My responsibilities for raising you are in the rearview mirror, and although I'd love to teach you what I've learned since you were in my safekeeping, I know that I cannot. The days for direct influence are over. I know you have a glimpse into the reasons for my activism. I feel that you understand them. Whether your life takes you closer into these concepts will be for you alone to decide.

In *The Parent's Tao Te Ching: Ancient Advice for Modern Parents*, the author William Martin implores us to "make the ordinary come alive" for our children, because "the extraordinary will take of itself." I may have missed the mark on some things, but I hope I've made some of the ordinary come alive for you. I hope I instilled a sense of unwavering love. The extraordinary did take care of itself, because you are an amazing human being.

Hindsight is always an incredible view.

Looking back, I now believe that the greatest gift we can give our children, is to teach them compassion: compassion for themselves and for all others. It's in this gift, that we provide the foundation upon which everything else we want for them is built.

Thank you for being an incredible gift to me.

With love always,

Mom

13

NOW I TEACH

It is a mistake for anyone to think he has lived too long in his old, unsatisfactory ways to make the great change. If you switch on the light in a dark room, it makes no difference how long it was dark, because the light will still shine. Be teachable. That is the whole secret.

— VERNON HOWARD

When your perception of the world takes a sharp 180, and your place on the planet seems, well, out of place, you're likely to be thrust into a strange new normal. You wonder with every cell in your body, how the people you know, respect, and love, can be so far removed from the epiphany you've had – an epiphany that seems effusively obvious to you now. The constant refusal of so many others to see the deep sanctity of life is a mind-boggling experience that you cannot wrap your mind around, no matter how hard you try. Nothing hurts a heart more than to live among people who can't understand what's inside it. Believe it or not, it can feel like drowning, or being buried alive. It is imperative to find some lifeline, or at least a strong rope to hold onto, so you can keep your head above water or land, and live to see a better day.

I've lost so many friends to the parallel universe of "what has always been." Family members refuse to bring up the subject at all, essentially redefining the parameters of our relationship, saying, although not necessarily in words: "I love you and we can communicate, just not about *that*."

Unfortunately, *that* is what I'm most passionate about. It has become the essence of who I am. Would you ask Yo-Yo Ma never to speak of a concerto he performed? Would you ask a physician on the brink of a new transplant procedure not to speak of her medical breakthrough? I believe that I've discovered the real tragedy of life – a woeful dearth of compassion -- and the solution – activated love that leads to renewed choices -- all at the same time. It's big news. I'm okay talking about the weather and the White House for just so long. But the elephant in the room is the fact that our entire species is facing extinction, the planet is dying, and animals are suffering. How are we not talking about that? How is fixing this not on the top of our to-do lists?

People eyeing my hat or tee shirt or necklace with the word vegan on it, instantly look away. There is nothing to fear about this word, but yet we all seem terrified by it. Even other yoga teachers confront me on social media, refuting my posts with every known excuse that their disciplined minds can come up with for not letting the animals off the hook. Vegans are drowning in an oblivious world, yet we swim to the surface, draw air into our lungs, and scream at the top of them: "Please stop! Please listen! And here's why."

My challenge has been to try to accept what is -- and for a seeker, empath, and justice-pursuing vegan – this has been a lot. I've sought refuge in two lifeboats to keep from going under. One is a deep commitment to animal liberation. The other is a steady spiritual practice that leads me back to my truest nature, enabling me to maintain a calmer and more compassionate outlook on the world around me. If I'm focused on writing, or coaching, or attending a march or a protest, I feel a sense of purpose in my life – a sense that I am doing something to change the course of history.

I'm no longer sure that happiness is always the state to strive for. I now believe that the goal is purpose, and from that purpose, joy can emerge.

Focused in both activism and spirituality, I find my bearings in a world that's off course and off-kilter. I strive to live in a state of gratitude. And I'm eternally grateful that I woke up to this deep understanding during my lifetime. Albert Einstein insisted that "those who have the privilege to know, have the duty to act." And so, we do. And so, I do.

But even when you think you've become aware, you're more often than not, still, in some ways, oblivious. I was aware of my sister-in-law's inability to acknowledge my nervous breakdown in the Chinese restaurant, all the while I was oblivious to the dead animals on my plate. I was aware of the concept of *ahimsa,* but at the same time I cozied up in my goose down jacket and sheepskin Uggs in the January freeze. I was aware of how much sacrifice it takes to care for a companion animal, oblivious to the fact that we had bought our sweet dog from a breeder, while so many beautiful souls are wasting away and dying in shelters and pounds, desperate for love, waiting for a good home, and in most cases facing euthanasia if that home did not materialize. I was aware of the pain I endured after my injury and still I was causing pain and misery with my personal choices. I was aware of the incredible change I made when I went vegan, but oblivious to the demands I made on people who were not ready or able to hear this message. I am brutally aware that I am brutally unaware. There's room for improvement only from this perspective.

The trick is to stay open, to stay curious, to want to understand more. The more we understand, the broader view we have, the better equipped we are to make decisions that serve both ourselves and the greater good. Without knowing, how are we even free to choose? We may think we're enjoying freedom, but until we dig a little deeper to know more, we remain indoctrinated with what we've been told to believe. Let's not kid ourselves: we've been taught what to think, what to believe, even what's "normal." And we're not free until we examine our thoughts and make sure they align with who we really are. Buddha said it best;

"Do not believe in anything simply because you have heard it.... But after observation and analysis, when you find that anything agrees with reason and is conducive to the good and benefit of one and all, then accept it and live up to it."

I teach veganism because I know how important a new paradigm is for all beings who live and die on this planet. We're clinging to old paradigms, outdated traditions – even when they're killing us and everything around us. We're watching Rome burn. I teach veganism because I believe it to be an oasis of justice, peace and love. This one powerful shift can repair broken bodies and broken hearts. It's done quite a bit to restructure mine.

Sometimes I dream of a new world. I can see it when I close my eyes. It's so beautiful there. I catch glimpses of it when I'm feeling really clear -- when I am determined not to be oblivious. In this world, the animals are free, and we are, too. We're not ill in body or mind. Everyone can breathe clean air and drink fresh water. No child is hungry. Our earth is renewed. Love abounds. We finally see and deeply understand the one thing that can free us from our own imprisonment: knowing we are not separate. We're not separate from one another, and we're not separate from the animals or the earth. If I hurt one, I hurt myself. If I heal one, I heal myself.

It's so simple, this going from oblivious to obvious. We are connected. The healing comes in knowing this, and living it.

ABOUT THE AUTHOR

Sande Nosonowitz
Sundara Vegan

Sande is a master-certified vegan coach, writer and educator. She penned a column for the Poughkeepsie Journal (*part of the USA TODAY network*) for three years called Living & Being Vegan and is the author of "OBLIVIOUS; A Vegan Memoir," as well as a compilation book, "Living & Being Vegan; How Veganism Heals Your Body, Mind and Spirit." Her multi-media presentation, *"How Veganism Heals,"* has been enjoyed by groups at venues such as The Mid-Hudson Regional Hospital, Dutchess Community College, The Omega Institute Staff Program, The DrawDown Environmental Program and The Fountains at Millbrook Community Education Series.

She's a proud co-founder of the Hudson Valley Vegfest held annually in New York State. Sande is also a certified yoga & meditation instructor who designs yoga & vegan-inspired jewelry that she lovingly calls, 'Hip & Holy Bling."

Sande teaches a full transition to veganism, including online modules, cooking classes, field trips to the grocery store and trips to the animal sanctuaries. An activist, teacher, student and animal lover, Sande lives in upstate New York with her vegan husband and plant-based yellow lab, Henry. You can learn more about Sande and Sundara Vegan's offerings on her website, www.sundaravegan.com.

facebook.com/sundaravegan
twitter.com/sundarajewel
instagram.com/sundarajewel

Made in the USA
Middletown, DE
21 September 2020